England

Endpapers Bluebell woods near Arlington, East Sussex.

Half title page A woodland scene in winter.

This page Ullswater at dusk.

Contents page Chatsworth, Derbyshire, is one of England's greatest stately homes.

This book was devised and produced by Multimedia Publications (UK) Ltd

Editor: Anthony J. Lambert
Production: Arnon Orbach
Design: John Strange and Associates
Picture Research: Moira Royse

ISBN 1 8317 2805 1

First published in the United States of America 1985 by Gallery Books, an imprint of W. H. Smith Publishers Inc., 112 Madison Avenue, New York, NY 10016.

Typeset by Flowery Typesetters Ltd.
Origination by CLG
Printed in Italy by Sagdos, Milan

England

Bryn Frank

GALLERY BOOKS
An Imprint of W. H. Smith Publishers Inc
112 Madison Avenue
New York City 10016

CONTENTS

CHAPTER 1

English Heritage

One man's charming English landscape is another's exciting glimpse into the past. Climb to the top of Maiden Hill in Dorset, a pre-Roman tribal stronghold, and you can enjoy a picnic with panoramic views. You might also see ghosts, because this is one of the most evocative hill forts in England, more than two miles around its perimeter.

Or stand on White Horse Hill, in Oxfordshire, surrounded by wind-ruffled long grass. Beside a symbolic horse carved out of the chalk hillside, you can hark back to the Iron Age, even as you watch brightly colored trains speeding by in the distance.

From what remains of Hadrian's Wall, in Northumberland — which is quite a lot — it is possible to look across many miles of open wild moorland that, give or take the occasional telephone pole, has not changed since the days when this was one of the remotest military postings in the Roman Empire. The Wall was built around 200 A.D., approximately 250 years after the Romans, under Julius Caesar, first appeared on the south coast of England.

A little bit of England goes a long way — back in time, that is. Just take a day trip into the country, in almost any direction from, say, London; it will be possible to discover a part-Saxon church, the remains of a Norman castle, or the outline (actually best seen from the air) of a deserted medieval village made uninhabitable by the Black Death or perhaps simply the lack of an adequate water supply. A 500-year-old half-timbered farmhouse that was once in the country is now embraced by a small town, a stable block that was originally an extension of a grand country mansion has

John Aubrey, historian and essayist, described Avebury as exceeding Stonehenge as a cathedral does a church. Originally a circle of 100 massive sarsen stones, Avebury was probably built around 2000-1500 BC, but as with Stonehenge its true origin is unknown.

become a holiday cottage complex. That redundant Victorian chapel has been transformed into a brass-rubbing center, which in itself is something of a bridge over troubled centuries. This parish church in the distance, graced by yew trees that were young when Charles I lost his head at the end of the English Civil War, had its tower *replaced* in 1500, on account of its "dangerous antiquity".

The past is all around us, and echoes of ancient times are heard not just among our great stately homes – built in a wealth of distinctive styles over the centuries – but in humbler buildings as well. The history of England is not just about kings, but cabbages too: visitors to the Ashmolean Museum, in Oxford, admire the "Alfred Jewel" that is inscribed in Latin, "Alfred had me made" (Alfred lived between 849 and 901); they can gaze within the Tower of London upon the execution block on which Anne Boleyn was beheaded about 700 years later. But on a more mundane level, farmers still occasionally unearth leather purses containing pathetic handfuls of medieval coins hidden in a field. Skeletons of presumably illegitimate babies have been known to turn up between the walls of moated Elizabethan manor houses, witnesses of the shaming of unworldly serving wenches.

It would be easy to categorize our ancestors as simple and untutored peasants, whose lives were "nasty, brutish and short". However, inconvenient details keep getting in the way, like the exquisitely carved roof of a cathedral whose intricate workmanship is only revealed by means of magnifying mirrors at ground level. Or take the great prehistoric edifice of Stonehenge, which was probably over two thousand years old when Hadrian's construction engineers shivered in the face of bitter winds blowing across the Northumbrian crags. Stonehenge's original purpose is still a mystery, but its construction, without the help of cranes and sophisticated tools, was an almost superhuman achievement.

Right The Gladstone Pottery Museum, Stoke-on-Trent, Staffordshire, has won prizes for its superb evocation of a vital part of England's industrial past. The presence of natural clay for pottery making, of coal for firing, water and cheap labor transformed the Midlands. In the background of the picture is a distinctive "bottle kiln": once they were dotted around Stoke, creating a landscape that will be familiar to readers of Arnold Bennett's novels, but only two or three remain.

Left Stokesay Castle, Shropshire. Probably the best preserved fortified manor house in the country, this has survived hundreds of years of English history. Built by the Norman family de Say (hence the name), it was impressively fortified by a rich wool merchant, Lawrence of Ludlow, in about 1290-1305. The interior and exterior timbering and other embellishments are remarkable.

Below Stonehenge, Wiltshire. Erected between about 2700 and 1300 BC, this is one of the most internationally famous monuments in Britain. Theories about its original purpose range from an open air observatory, to an elaborate sacrificial site: the truth may never be known, but certainly the axis aligns exactly with the sunrise on June 21, the longest day in the year.

Castles, great houses, abbeys and cathedrals, many of them over a thousand years old, are dotted around England like milestones for the convenience of the historian and the delight of the visitor. Towns and villages, often incredibly well preserved, provide clues to the way of life of ordinary people. Things were not necessarily as uncomfortable as we used to think. The Romans, for example, knew how to make plate glass, and many post-Roman castles were glazed and probably much more comfortable to live in than they are usually given credit for. As longer periods of peace enabled castles to be regarded as homes first and defense works second, there was time and money for such refinements as draft-excluding tapestries, loose and therefore disposable matting on the floors, murals and brightly painted woodwork.

Some houses are preserved as in aspic, perfect specimens of their period. Some have grown haphazardly over the years, much enriched by associations with momentous events or with artists and statesmen: Shakespeare is thought to have

hunted deer in Charlecote Park, Warwickshire; there is a mulberry tree in John Milton's house in Buckinghamshire that was certainly alive when he lived there; and Winston Churchill's country seat in Chartwell, Kent, has fish in the pond that are direct descendants of those he took special pleasure in feeding by hand.

There are certain eras in English history which romantics hark back to. One is the first Elizabethan age, marvelously well documented, remembered in song, drama and painting. Although it was a brilliant period, for some people the Elizabethans are too far away: they prefer the Jacobean or the Georgian and the emergence of an Age of Elegance – the time of Handel and of Gainsborough, of Capability Brown and the great eighteenth-century architects.

A good history book and a sharp eye will suffice for some, but bridging the gap for most of us between the eighteenth century and the present day are several remarkable open air museums, carefully reconstructed glimpses of the past. In the north of England is the Beamish Open Air Museum, where the lives of early coal miners, railway

Opposite above Little Moreton Hall, Cheshire. Frequently seen on calendars and candy boxes, this is the best known and one of the best preserved half-timbered houses in England. It is the result of three generations of extensions and "improvements" of the Moreton family, and was originally built, when wood was plentiful, by William Moreton at the end of the fifteenth century.

Opposite below The Radcliffe Camera, Oxford (one of the reading rooms of the Bodleian library), seen from inside All Souls' College. All Souls was founded by Henry Chichele in 1437 to commemorate Henry V and all those who were killed at the battle of Agincourt. It does not have undergraduate members but graduate fellows elected for their academic prowess. It is an outstandingly elegant college even in Oxford terms.

Below Willy Lott's Cottage, Flatford Mill, Suffolk. In the very heart of soft and gentle "Constable country", close to the Essex border, and about a mile south of East Bergholt, this world-famous building stands on the north bank of the River Stour. One of the watermills owned by John Constable's father (Willy Lott was a tenant), it figures in several Constable paintings.

Blenheim Palace, Oxfordshire, was conferred on John Churchill, 1st Duke of Marlborough, by a grateful nation for his defeat of Louis XIV at the battle of Blenheim in 1704. The great house was originally to be designed by Christopher Wren, but it was Sir John Vanbrugh who created it between 1705 and 1722. The park spreads to about 2,500 acres

workers and mill hands are contrasted with the wealth of the land-owning aristocracy. Not far from the Welsh border, in Shropshire, is the Ironbridge Gorge Museum, situated in what has been called the cradle of the Industrial Revolution. One does not need a time machine: warehouses, blast furnaces, china works, canals and the world's first iron bridge, over the Severn Gorge, are rich in accessible memories of a teeming period in the history of England.

Historians seldom refer to the "weaker sex". In legendary terms they may point to Queen Boudicca, who almost defeated the Roman invaders. In factual terms they hark back to Elizabeth I and, less than a hundred years ago, to Queen Victoria. Both Elizabeth and Victoria had long reigns during periods of great prosperity. The popularity of Victoriana in architecture, furniture and design is comparatively recent, but no less thorough. The Victorians in their time loved to hark back to "Merrie England", and idealized portraits of happy peasantry grace many a nineteenth-century Town Hall. This is an enthusiam shared by the twentieth century, in which there is much dressing up in traditional costumes by off-duty bank workers and accountants, performing bizarre rituals, livening up market places and holiday fairs. For England's past is not just invested in material objects, however beautiful; the medieval world is alive and well. In Abbots Bromley for example, they perform a Horn Dance, supposedly a glorified fertility rite, that is one of the longest surviving customs in Europe. At Allendale, in Northumberland, on January 1, men carry barrels of blazing tar on their heads to the market place, in an English version of Scotland's "first footing", a New Year ritual. It has much to do with surviving the winter and looking forward to a fresh new dawn.

The falconer on the green, the extrovert dressed up as Henry VIII at a "medieval banquet", the pre-lunch game of croquet you may be offered if you spend the weekend in a hotel may be commercial gimmicks but they do have their place in the scheme of things. Maypole dancing is a skill acquired by primary school children in rural areas, museums are no longer regarded as "old hat", and history books frequently become best sellers. A fascination with centenaries of dramatic events is evidence of a huge interest in history and an increased awareness of the debt that is owed to previous centuries.

Right Lincoln Cathedral, Lincolnshire. Built on a steep hill this 700-year-old cathedral, which is the third largest in England, is a classic Lincolnshire landmark, especially when floodlit. Though created piecemeal, the cathedral seems remarkably harmonious. Especially important are the east window, Wren's library — containing the first edition of *Paradise Lost* and *Don Quixote* and one of only four copies of the Magna Carta.

Far right Brougham Castle, Cumbria, lies on the pleasant, green unspectacular side of the county often overlooked by people who know only the Lake District. It was built in the 1170s, and was acquired by the wealthy Lady Ann Clifford in the seventeenth century. Her passion was to restore ancient castles, and she died at Brougham at the age of eighty-nine in 1676.

Below The Iron Bridge, Ironbridge, Shropshire. The first structure of its kind in the world, it symbolizes the Industrial Revolution in England. The forerunner of today's steel-framed buildings, the bridge — completed in 1779 — has a single 100ft arch, and rises 45ft above the River Severn. No bolts were used: sections were fitted together as if of wood, with shoulder and dovetail joints.

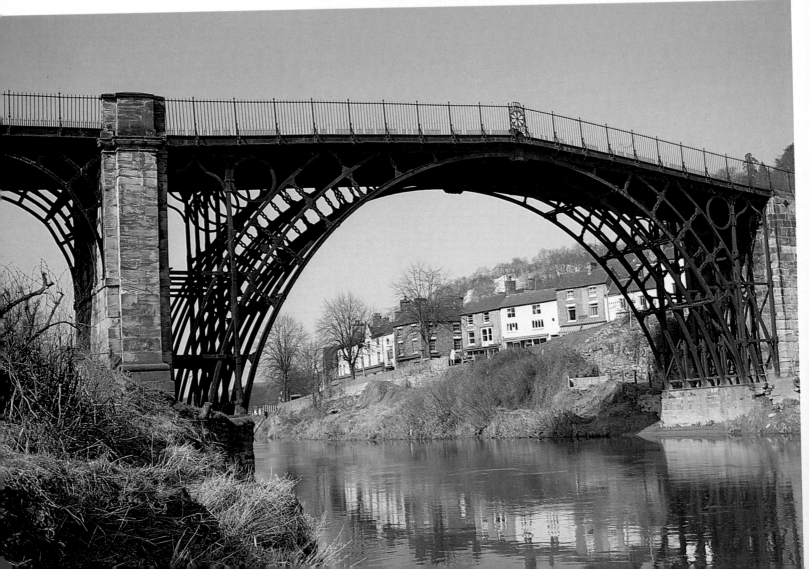

Right Celebrating Britain's "Tudor Heritage" at Hever Castle, Kent. Henry VIII confiscated the mainly thirteenth-century castle from the family of Anne Boleyn after her execution and later gave it to Anne of Cleves, his fourth wife — supposedly to compensate for divorcing her soon after their marriage in 1540. The gardens are spectacular, including a maze and a garden displaying Italian columns, statues and busts.

Below May Day, Knutsford, Cheshire. May Day was originally "Beltane", during which the Celts marked the beginning of summer with bonfires in the sun's honor. Later, people collected wild flowers and various types of greenery from the hedgerows and decorated their homes with that. Maypole dancing, as here, originated with dances round white hawthorn — another spring fertility symbol.

Left Morris dancing at Axbridge, Somerset. Many a pub car park is enlivened by teams of Morris dancers, whose name is probably derived from the word "Moorish" — meaning, at one time, all that was strange and rather scary. Their dance may be traced back to an elaborate fertility rite, with much symbolism but not necessarily, among the dancers, a lot of natural rhythm.

Below Montacute House, Somerset, is a typically dominant and awe-inspiring Elizabethan mansion. Built by Sir Edward Phelps between 1580 and 1600, the house contains paintings on loan from the National Portrait Gallery as well as fine furniture and tapestries. Phelps was Speaker at the House of Commons in 1604 and prosecutor at the trial of Guy Fawkes in 1605. The name comes from the Latin *mons acutus,* or steep hill.

The English Village

Industrialists retire to them, expatriates dream of them, and rock stars buy walled properties on their outskirts. They are English villages, sometimes slumbering under great oaks, copper beeches or chestnuts, sometimes straggling prettily along the banks of a rippling stream or the sides of a valley, but occasionally so adversely affected by heavy trucks that older buildings may literally fall to pieces.

The ideal English village exists only in the imagination. Or does it? Occasionally a newspaper or magazine initiates a search for the perfect village. Its pub will probably be a thatched and whitewashed showpiece, and almost certainly close to the parish church. Unless, that is, this ideal village happens to be one where the houses have been resited to satisfy the whim of a wealthy eighteenth-century landlord and only the church remains, alone in a field, in its original position. Strange hillocks and mounds around it will indicate where the original village was sited.

In an increasingly secular society the village church will have a peculiar role to play. Still a place of worship but noticeably busiest at nostalgic times like Christmas and Easter, it will be much visited by passing strangers and also play a nonreligious role in the life of the community. There will be flower festivals, recitals – if the old organ is up to it – by a visiting musician, conducted talks by the vicar about the Victorian stained glass.

The winding, cobbled and venerable Gold Hill, Shaftesbury, Dorset, is one of the most photographed streets in the West Country. At its top, near St. Peter's Church, is a unique button museum (the town was widely known for its button manufacturing). It is worth remembering that when Gold Hill was a busy street, all water used had to be carted up from below.

The churchyard of nostalgic dreams will contain lichened headstones standing at drunken angles amid sheep-cropped grass, for anything *too* manicured smacks of suburbia. Overhung with yew trees that the churchwarden fondly believes are 500 years old (they *can* live to be a thousand), the churchyard will be adjacent to a row of pastel colored cottages set off by hollyhocks and snapdragons.

A fantasy village may be of Cotswold limestone, of Devon cob (basically clay mixed with gravel and straw), of Kentish brick and half-timbering, of white-painted Sussex weatherboard. For dreamers with family roots or memories of happy holidays in East Anglia, the cottages will be plaster stuccoed and pale pink: traditionally that pink was derived from mixing whitewash with pig's blood, a by-product of an important Suffolk industry, which was pig farming. Goats, not pigs, will be tethered on the grassy verges that border the lane that leads down to the village green from Church Cottages. A cricket match will be in progress on the green.

There are villages in England that, attractive though they may be, are unsettling for outsiders because they are scattered, shapeless, sprawling places that lack a green. Goathland, in North Yorkshire, for example, has a whole series of greens, and nobody really knows which is the main one; Nenthead, on the eastern edge of Cumbria, is a scattered hillside settlement without a focal point.

On the village green the cricket match is interrupted for tea (cynics will say: "interrupted by rain"). The clink of tea cups and the slicing of cucumbers to make sandwiches are sounds as nostalgic as the call of the wood pigeon or, much rarer, cuckoo. Some village greens have survived being dissected by main roads, and the best of them may resemble common heathland rather than the manicured lawns idealized on candy boxes.

Village greens may set off elegant churches to advantage, as at Long Melford, in Suffolk. Sometimes they used to have practical value, as at Elsdon, in Northumberland, where all the

Far left Bosmere Mill, Needham Market, Suffolk. The great height of many eighteenth-century watermills is due to the system whereby hoisting gear raised grain to a storage loft at the highest level, from where it passed by means of gravity to the grinding floor below. The cantilevered structure at the top, called a "lucam", housed the hoist.

Below In the early 1960s Castle Combe, Wiltshire, was chosen as "the prettiest village in England." Almost too-good-to-be-true, it is nevertheless a living community, composed mainly of honey-colored Cotswold stone. The original manor house is now a hotel, the parish church was endowed in the fifteenth century by wealthy local businessmen.

Below These sixteenth- and seventeenth-century timber-framed houses at Chiddingstone, West Sussex, and owned by the National Trust, are perfect examples of their period and are often used as part of a film set. Opposite there is the yew-shaded churchyard. The real gem is the Long House, which is about 500 years old. The style of building is typical of the Kentish Weald: half-timbering with brick, tile hangings, gables and steeply pitched roof.

passageways between houses could be sealed off and cattle corralled on the green when cattle thieves were about on the wild fells that then, as now, characterize the Scottish-English border country.

Many village greens have incorporated a village pond, which may have been used to stock fish, or even to drown suspected witches, but is now merely decorative.

Beside the green may be a blacksmith's shop, still in business after hundreds of years, though now making wrought-iron gates for weekend cottage owners instead of plowshares. The village mailman stands by his bike to watch the cricket, but not long enough for electric bills to arrive late. The village shop behind him may stock too much powdered milk and frozen vegetables for our taste, but at least it is still surviving.

Travel writers and adventurous vacationers like to pick their top ten or dozen villages. Some places crop up again and again. Often the lists include the pretty limestone village of Blanchland, on the boundary between County Durham and Northumberland. The name derives from the White Friars who had an abbey here when border raids inflicted by Scottish cattle thieves were at their peak in the fourteenth and fifteenth centuries. It is said that because one raid, in 1327, took place in the autumnal mist that tends to cloak the village, lying as it does below a steep escarpment and on the banks of the River Derwent, the raiders were prevented from discovering the abbey and its worldly treasures. But the monks celebrated their deliverance too soon by sounding the bells, and the raiders returned.

Left Old Minehead, Somerset, is hidden away amid the more sprawling, heavily commercialized holiday resort the town has become: look for it at the western end of the town, on the hillside. The steps in the picture lead up to the partly fourteenth-, partly fifteenth-century church. Nearby is the pretty, old harbor — reminiscent of the days when Minehead was an important trading center.

Below Water Lane, Lavenham, Suffolk: a happy marriage of domestic architecture of different periods in a small town (some call it a large village) that is a model of sympathetic conservation. One reason Lavenham has stayed intact is that its wealth from the fifteenth- and sixteenth-century wool trade declined, and there was no money for "modernization and improvement".

Far right Church Lane, Ledbury, Hereford and Worcester. A classic view of Church Lane, enhanced by hanging baskets, which is just one notable street in a charming and often overlooked town that is particularly notable for its seventeenth-century architecture and its hostelries: "The Prince of Wales" is just one of at least three ancient pubs. The poet John Masefield was born in the town in 1878.

Below The village shop is, if not "alive and well", surviving. But delightfully old fashioned fronts often hide a modern interior and refrigerated display cabinets. Sometimes the shop doubles as a post office, with guaranteed income, or belongs to a marketing co-operative. This shop, with an attractive Victorian window, is in Sutton Courtenay, Oxfordshire.

Also stone built, but much more scattered than Blanchland, as if its houses had been shaken from some celestial pepper pot, is the village of Elterwater, close to Elter Water, one of the least known lakes in the Lake District. Those lucky sightseers who have found Elterwater—one suspects by chance—may often be discovered picnicking on one of the unofficial, unkempt village greens. But not all England's favored villages are "sermons in stone." Red brick, which people who have never seen a Christopher Wren country house or a handsome garden wall with summer evening sunlight on it, do not appreciate until they have seen it for themselves, is common in much of the south of England and the Midlands: unpretentious slate roofs, a red brick terrace under a scudding April sky, are sights for sore eyes. Perhaps the best villages are those that combine a whole range of architectural styles and building materials while remaining harmonious and carefully treated.

Ashwell, in Hertfordshire, is one such. With a well tended churchyard, houses that are half-timbered here, partly in stone there, some built of highly decorative red brick of different sizes and hues, some pastel colored and rendered, it benefits greatly from a superb local museum. Ashwell has been described as "a triumphant survivor" because of the way it has coped with the vicissitudes of nearly a thousand years.

Sometimes the most worthwhile villages are those off the beaten track and rarely encountered by tourists. Kimbolton, in Cambridgeshire, and Pleshey, in Essex, both mainly of brick, are two examples of attractive places only a couple of hours' drive from London that are comparatively little visited. Pleshey, whose "ey" probably denotes that Anglo-Saxons built on drained land, has very few remains of its Norman castle except for a magnificent man made mound. Kimbolton is dominated at one end of its pretty high street by a boys' school, and it is easy to imagine pupils in the early

nineteenth century climbing down from stagecoaches stopped outside any of the coaching inns that used to exist here but are now mainly private houses.

You could stick a pin in a map of rural England and, nine times out of ten, land on a village of much interest. Even if its history is swamped by modern development or ravaged by traffic, hundreds of years of history lie just under the surface. You might pinpoint a gem, a black and white "magpie" village like Weobley, in Hereford and Worcester, or leafy Fotheringhay, in whose castle Mary Queen of Scots was beheaded at 8 a.m. on February 8, 1587, or the two Slaughters, Upper and Lower, in Gloucestershire. Upper Slaughter, being further away from the main road, more scattered and wooded, is less well known, while Lower Slaughter is a honeypot for painters and weekend drivers. The

"Slaughter" incidentally, has nothing to do with murder and mayhem but probably refers to a prominent local family who were called de Slochter.

How do we know for sure that the traditional English village really is alive and well? For one thing, modern housing developments ape it. Houses for rising young executives are clustered around a bit of greenery, attached "cottages" are built in slightly different styles to complement each other, hanging baskets are installed by the speculative builder, gables and wicker fences are part of the original specification.

It is not exactly "back to the land," but it is certainly "back to the village," something which is reflected in a revival in the fortunes of some inner cities. For they too are often a collection of villages. Life, it seems, is much better like that.

Below Midhurst, West Sussex, lies on the River Rother. The vicissitudes of history have scarcely affected the pleasant town. H. G. Wells was a pupil at the originally seventeenth-century grammar school, and the remains of Cowdray House, a Tudor mansion destroyed by fire in 1793, can be seen in Cowdray Park. The latter is probably best known for the polo matches played there, occasionally involving the Prince of Wales.

Left Thatching at Merton, Devon. This ancient craft, involving either the very resilient Norfolk reed or the less long lasting (but some say more attractive) West Country straw, is enjoying a revival. Master thatchers usually have their own "trade mark" — so look out for a decorative peacock, rabbit or geometric shape on top of a thatched roof.

Below Boxford Mill, about 5 miles from Newbury, Berkshire, is just one of the neat and tidy buildings in Boxford village.
Perhaps the most famous resident of the village was a Quaker called Oliver, who refused to pay his tythes, and is remembered at Oliver's House, by the church gate. Most unusually, the parish church has a barrel organ.

Heptonstall, West Yorkshire, was left behind by the Industrial Revolution of the late eigthteenth century, and it was Hebden Bridge, down in the valley, that prospered. A network of narrow streets embraces many memories of the past: a seventeenth-century grammar school, the oldest Methodist Chapel in the world that is still in use, and relics of the Civil War.

Left Preparing a cake, of "cheese", during cider making. Finding local cider is one of the bonuses of a West Country visit — and we use the term "West Country" loosely as Hereford and Worcester is also a major cider producing area. Some cider enthusiasts say that the more rough and ready the product, the more authentic it is.

Far left The cottage garden. By a curious historical link, such gardens originated after the Dissolution of the Monasteries in about 1530: for herbs previously grown in those monasteries were no longer available, and people began to grow their own. Though very pretty now, everything had a purpose. Even topiary was used for laying out washing to dry.

Below Once, every village blacksmith generally shod horses (doubling up as a farrier) as well as repairing and making plows and other essential farm implements. Many forges are still in use, often as workshops in which mainly decorative wrought ironwork is produced, though garden gates and fire grates are commonly made too, and, in particular, curlicued house-names.

CHAPTER 3

Literary Landscapes

A bleak moor that inspired Emily Brontë to some of the most dramatic passages in her novel *Wuthering Heights* is not just a moor. A stone where William Wordsworth liked to sit and contemplate his beloved Rydal Water is not merely any old bit of rock. A glorified shed where George Bernard Shaw enjoyed writing on the grounds of his house in Ayot St. Lawrence, in Hertfordshire, is not just any shed (aside from the fact that it did and does revolve, in order to catch as much sunlight through its window as possible).

Eastwood, in Nottinghamshire, where D. H. Lawrence was born and spent his childhood, may be seen as a blot on the landscape by the casual passerby. The scrubby, faded rural hinterland of this one-time mining community is, however, much enhanced by its association with certain Lawrence novels – particularly *Sons and Lovers*. The wide open fields, under what Alfred Lord Tennyson referred to as "yonder living blue" still attracts widely read travelers to rural Lincolnshire, and particularly to the Lincolnshire Wolds, even though they may have been warned that the county is "as flat as a board" (which is not how Tennyson described it). The poet's home at Somersby is not open to the public, but the leafy lane that passes it, from where one can see open fields through sun dappled trees, is a delight in itself as well as part of the Tennyson myth.

You do not have to be a literature major to get a thrill from a country churchyard as "the curfew tolls the knell of parting day" — Gray's "Elegy" was partly inspired by Stoke Poges Church — or a rectory in wooded parkland that might have stepped right out of the pages of a Jane Austen novel. People

Jane Austen would certainly have known the parish church at Chawton, Hampshire. Her house here is open to the public, almost unaltered since she lived there.

Right Inside William Wordsworth's study at Dove Cottage, Grasmere, shrine for lovers of his poetry from all over the world. We may draw a veil over the fact that none in a hundred of them will be able to quote more than a line from any Wordsworth poem. William lived here for nine years at the very height of his inspiration, making this into one of England's foremost literary shrines.

Below Grasmere in winter. Were it not for the associations with Wordsworth this might have remained off the beaten track, to be discovered only by connoisseurs of the lesser lakes. As it is, it throngs with visitors — though not (and this is a hint to people who want to get the true flavor of the lakes and feel something of Wordsworth's rare harmony with the natural world) in winter.

are known to travel hundreds of miles to visit a house or castle, and sometimes much more mundane spots, associated with famous writers. Where such a place is interesting in its own right, it becomes a double bonus. So Lawrence Sterne's house in Coxwold, North Yorkshire, where he lived with his faithful cat and wrote *Tristram Shandy*, is open to the public and delightful. So is the house in which Dr Johnson was born in Lichfield, Staffordshire, in 1709, a well maintained echo of the past in which it is easy to imagine the burly doctor negotiating steep and narrow stairs.

Some corners of England are so closely associated with literary figures that they take the writer's name. Say "Shakespeare country" and most people, whether or not they have ever seen a Shakespeare play, will have a rough inkling that you are referring to what is either unromantically called the Midlands, or more romantically, the "Heart of England" – or at least a part of it. The Lake District is so indelibly linked with Wordsworth and the other Romantic poets that one enterprising hotelier recently put up a sign in a road outside his inn which read "Wordsworth did not sleep here." The real focal point for Wordsworthians is Grasmere, where they find Dove Cottage and the Wordsworth Museum. Wordsworth lived at Dove Cottage between 1799 and 1808, and it was here that most of his best known poetry was written. He was buried in the church at Grasmere and his larger home, "up the road" at Rydal Mount, was opened to the public in 1970, the bi-centenary of his birth. Much less well known but well worth a detour is Cockermouth, Wordsworth's birthplace, which provides a good excuse for visiting one of the most attractive Cumbrian towns.

There is more to the Lakeland literary tradition than Wordsworth however. Beatrix Potter, born in 1866, the creator of animal fantasies that began with *The Tale of*

Below The Moot Hall, Elstow, Bedfordshire, is more or less the same as it was when John Bunyan, author of *The Pilgrim's Progress,* who was born in the adjoining parish in 1628, lived in the village. At one time there were shops on the ground floor. The building may originally have been used to house guests of the nearby abbey.

Peter Rabbit and have never been out of print, lived in Hilltop, near Sawrey, in a house that is also open to the public, amid dramatic countryside. The house is now owned by the National Trust.

Beatrix Potter was partially contemporary with Thomas Hardy, who always considered himself a much better poet than novelist, but whose novels, generally more popular than his poems, are read today. He made "Wessex" as much his own as Wordsworth, Coleridge, and De Quincey did the Lakes.

Hardy lived in Dorset most of his life. This southerly county, as well as neighboring parts of Devon, Wiltshire and Hampshire, provided the setting for so many places that are identifiable with the help of the original story and a good map. For example, Blandford Forum became Hardy's Shottsford Forum, Dorchester became Casterbridge, Tolpuddle became Weatherbury, and Weymouth became Budmouth Regis. Hardy was born in Higher Bockhampton in a traditional thatched cottage set amidst a pretty garden. As a young architect one of his first assignments was to restore the church at St. Juliot in Cornwall, and it was there that he met his wife to be.

If Hardy is still well read, almost everything that the Brontë sisters wrote has remained in print, and some of their books have always been best sellers, a phenomenon no doubt aided by the consistent popularity of television and film adaptations of their work. So it is not surprising that the Brontë Parsonage in Haworth, West Yorkshire, is at the top of the Yorkshire and Humberside Tourist Board's list of popular houses.

Above left Perfectly situated on a slight incline, the parish church of St. Michael and All Angels at Hawkshead, Cumbria, was well known to William Wordsworth: he liked to sit outside in the churchyard by the east wall. The interior of the church is notable for the quality of its decorative arch and pillar painting.

Left Rydal Water is more a tarn than a lake. Edged with reeds, and much sought after by visiting fishermen, it rightly makes no concessions to commercialism, and indeed there are scarcely any lay-bys or parking spaces. Dominating this "lesser lake" are the heights of Loughrigg and Nab Scar.

Right Rydal Mount, where Wordsworth lived between 1813 and his death in 1850, is much more substantial than Dove Cottage, and it really has fewer direct literary associations. It was at Rydal that Wordsworth was lionized, and where he enjoyed a ripe old celebrity: he died at the age of eighty.

Right Mary Arden's House, Wilmcote, near Stratford-upon-Avon, Warwickshire. Mary Arden was the mother of William Shakespeare, and the playwright would have courted Ann Hathaway — properly chaperoned — by the fireside. This house appeals greatly, perhaps because, unlike the other "Shakespeare properties" it is out of town and little affected by the ravages of the twentieth century.

Below Dove Cottage, Grasmere. Home of William and Dorothy Wordsworth, it was in this modest cottage that most of the poet's best work was produced. It was inspired both by his experiences across the Channel when caught up in the French Revolution and the lakeland scenery that must have seemed a million miles from London.

The Five Towns of Arnold Bennett's novels and short stories – Bennett's birthplace is now a café – attract visitors not just on account of the superb industrial archeology, notably the Gladstone Museum, but because of the continuing fondness readers have for Bennett's books and plays, peopled as they are with portly bankers and thrusting young entrepreneurs grabbing their share of the tremendous wealth that was generated here from the end of the eighteenth century.

Hardly industrialized but still little regarded is Northamptonshire, the haunt of the nineteenth-century poet John Clare, who has never been a household word but who may yet come into his own. The rolling brown farmland and narrow roads that seem to lead nowhere are reminiscent for anyone who has come across John Clare with his essentially sad but minutely observed poetry. At least he is easier to come to terms with than Dickens or Jane Austen, because both of those writers,

among others, are closely linked with so many places that literary associations are hard to pin down neatly. It is probably easier to deal with writers and poets associated with comparatively specific places. Thus, A. E. Housman is the voice of rural Shropshire (much bleaker than many people think), John Bunyan is the only well known literary figure to come out of Bedfordshire, Charles Kingsley, author of *The Water Babies*, is likely to be thought of by librarians, booksellers and well read children when anyone mentions Clovelly or Bideford in Devon.

Nostalgia-through-literature and an enhanced appreciation of the English landscape is not necessarily a matter of the past. No novelist or poet has ever done so much for London's suburban counties as the late Sir John Betjeman, and the character of Yorkshire has been evocatively portrayed by James Herriot whose books, about veterinary surgeons between the wars, sell in their hundreds of thousands.

Below Lyme Regis, Dorset, was the favorite seaside resort of Jane Austen, and the steeply banked, tightly packed little place still has terraces of houses unchanged since her time. The town is mentioned in *Persuasion*. It is also the home town of novelist John Fowles, whose best-selling novel *The French Lieutenant's Woman* is set in Lyme Regis.

Right Thomas Hardy was born in 1840 and grew up in a modest cottage at Higher Bockhampton that had been built by his grandfather in 1800. Here the novelist, who really thought of himself as a poet, wrote *Under the Greenwood Tree* and *Far From The Madding Crowd*. He had come here to write after abandoning his career as an architect.

Far right Henley on Thames, Oxfordshire. The Thames has been the inspiration of many writers, among them Wordsworth, Spenser and Dickens. Upstream, where the pace of life seems more gentle and there is time to feed the swans, there are abiding memories of Jerome K. Jerome (author of *Three Men In A Boat*) and Kenneth Grahame (author of *Wind in the Willows*), among others.

Below The Brontë connection has put the gritty, higgledy-piggledy West Yorkshire town of Haworth on the tourist map. Patrick Brontë, father of Emily, Charlotte and Anne and of Branwell, who lived in their shadow, was rector at the parish church. The Brontë Parsonage, the family home that stands close by, is open to the public: avoid peak summer periods, as it is so popular.

Left The Mermaid Inn, Rye, is an English classic of abut 1420. At the top of a steep, cobbled street in this very popular, but largely unspoilt town, its low-beamed rooms and cosy paneled interior exudes the atmosphere of a bygone age. It was once notorious as a haunt of smugglers who learnt to take advantage of local sea mists and sand banks.

Below Charles Dickens spent his honeymoon in 1836 in the village of Chalk, in Kent. The original cottage in which he stayed no longer exists, but a photograph of it can be seen at the Dickens House in Doughty Street, London. The cottage in this photograph is generally taken to be an almost identical building.

CHAPTER 4

National Parks

A rash of speculative building between the wars caused much concern to an increasing number of people who cared deeply for the English countryside. They had also pressed for better public access to wild areas of mountain and moorland – something that is now taken for granted. Happily, within five years of the end of the Second World War, the equivalent of what is now the Countryside Commission was responsible for setting up ten National Parks, which cover 3600 square miles of England.

Compared with Wales's National Parks, England's tend to be inland rather than coastal but three in England – Exmoor, North Yorks Moors and the Lake District – are much enhanced by coastal encounters, emphasizing the close relationship in a comparatively small island between sea and countryside.

The National Parks are the most beautiful and unspoilt expanses of open countryside in England, as are the less rigidly controlled but still well protected areas of Outstanding Natural Beauty, of which there are 30.

Mainly composed of sweeping downland, valleys and fells, cliffs and shoreline, the National Parks also embrace living communities and fully fledged towns. Indeed, those villages and towns which lie within the National Park boundaries often have a special quality about them. Though sometimes rather self-consciously pretty and privileged, for they are never allowed to decay, they can make an ideal introduction to England for overseas visitors. Among the most photographed and visited are Keswick and Windermere in the Lake

In the heart of Northumberland's Roman Wall country, Crag Lough lies on the Whin Sill. The views from these crags can have changed little since the Roman legionnaires paced the ramparts and scanned the northern horizon for Pictish invaders.

Right Familiar to walkers in Wharfedale, the best of the little town of Grassington is clustered round its market square, a haven from the high-lying often bleak and inhospitable country around. Stone and water are the two most distinctive features of the Yorkshire Dales landscape hereabouts, and residents of industrial West Yorkshire are the most frequent visitors to this particular National Park.

Below The River Greta near Ingleton in the Yorkshire Dales National Park. A few miles north of Settle, this part of the country is crossed by packhorse trails, along which was carried coal mined at Ingleton. More dramatically, the route of the Settle to Carlisle railway runs nearby: by far the most spectacular on the whole of the British Rail network.

District, Bakewell in the Peak District, Hawes and Grassington in the Yorkshire Dales, Chagford and Lynton in Dartmoor and Exmoor respectively.

The setting up of the National Parks in 1950, coming no fewer than 78 years after the creation of America's first, which was the Yellowstone National Park (as big, incidentally, as all England's seven parks put together) was to draw attention to comparatively little-known parts of Britain and to boost the popularity of regions that were already household names. Dartmoor, for example, had long been famous for its prison, its swirling mists and its massive granite tors; the Lake District had been a tourist honeypot almost since the time Wordsworth and the Romantic poets claimed it as their own. But the Peak District, the first Park to be operative and now the most heavily visited, was little known except locally. And Exmoor, populated by red deer and dramatically bordered by the Bristol Channel, has remained comparatively unexplored even today.

Even people who claim to be familiar with Yorkshire may not know the difference between the North York Moors and the Yorkshire Dales parks. The first distinction is that one lies east of the Hambleton Hills, the other west, where it is traversed by the Pennine Way, though much more important for the average country lover is their difference in character: the North York Moors park is, typically, composed of brown rolling windswept moorland that climaxes in a rugged weatherbeaten sandstone coastline. The Moors are predominantly brown, purple and gold, characterized in places by tiny, cheek-by-jowl red-roofed villages reaching down precipitate narrow lanes barely wide enough for one car let alone tour buses, by the skeletal ruins of once proud monastic buildings – notably Rievaulx, Byland and Mount Grace. In the fishing villages of Robin Hood's Bay and Staithes, every inch of available space between the cliffs is occupied by tiny-roomed houses, of three or even four storeys.

Below Close to the border of County Durham and Cumbria, "High Cup Nick" lies on the Great Whin Sill that dominates much of the North Country's high ground. About 5 miles north east of Appleby, this is beautiful countryside that benefits greatly from being bypassed by the majority of tourists. Villages are few, towns are almost non-existent, but the terrain is not inaccessible.

The Yorkshire Dales National Park is generally a more fertile, more intensively farmed and prosperous marriage of mountain, valley and moorland, intersected by fast flowing rivers and distinguished by gritstone summits of peaks that challenge climbers. Most famous are the Three Peaks – Ingleborough, Whernside and Pen-y-Ghent – all three of which are linked by the Pennine Way. There are several dramatic waterfalls, among the best known being Hardraw and Aysgarth, and some impressive monuments to the past, notably Bolton Castle, dominating peaceful Wensleydale and Bolton Priory.

The county of Northumberland, let alone the Northumberland National Park, is largely unknown except to its inhabitants. Stretching bleakly but beautifully south of the Scottish border, its hillsides partially clothed by Forestry Commission woods, the Park includes within its boundaries the 2700 foot high Cheviot. This is the only National Park to have nothing remotely approaching a town. Some stretches of the park are managed by the Forestry Commission, which gives many hills the increasingly familiar dark green, heavily wooded appearance that some people object to for its uniformity. This is most apparent around the Kielder Forest, where the creation of a massive reservoir flooded a valley that, it has to be admitted, was rarely explored by visitors, and brought new life to what for tourists was a wilderness. For anglers, water skiers and sailors now have the chance to appreciate that there is more to rural Northumberland than watching for curlews (the curlew is the Northumberland National Park's symbol) and trying to find a rare café in which to escape from the rain.

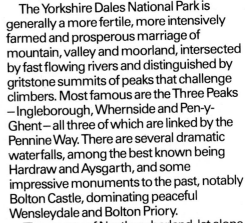

Above left Pen-y-Ghent is probably the best known peak in the Yorkshire Dales National Park, and at 2273ft, it is a great landmark on the 250-mile-long Pennine Way. Reached most easily from the straggling moorland village of Horton-in-Ribblesdale, it is a magnet for hikers and climbers. This is also potholing country: dangerous but fascinating.

Left The River Swale, near the village of Keld, before it reaches the most distinguished place on its course, which is Richmond.

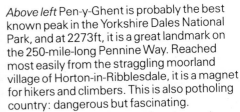

Right The Roman Wall was much more elaborate than anything of the kind built elsewhere in Europe. Though substantial remains are admired and even walked along by today's visitors, the original specifications were much more impressive. There was a ditch 27ft wide and nearly 10ft deep, the wall itself was over 7ft wide, and the walkway was 15ft above ground.

Opposite above Perhaps the most famous village in Lakeland, Watendlath is connected to Borrowdale by a narrow road. Though access by car is thus feasible, this is essentially walking country (though not strenuously so). The few whitewashed houses do not detract from the scene, blending well with the natural stone.

Opposite below All too many Lakeland visitors are bounded by main roads and official car parks. This view of peaks above Eskdale is normally vouchsafed only to energetic walkers, and even then only when the unpredictable Lakeland weather is fine and clear. Perhaps best known among tourists for the miniature railway that links it to the coast at Ravenglass, Eskdale lies on the west side of the region.

Below Ingleborough Fell, on the western side of the central Pennines, rises to 2350ft. It is typical limestone "karst" country (the name is originally Yugoslavian), characterized by caves, riverless valleys, underground streams and caverns. Much of this sort of terrain is regarded as unsafe for sheep to graze — especially when winter snows hide crevices and ditches.

The Northumberland National Park is the most sparsely inhabited of the seven in England, and extends to the very ramparts of the Great Wall which the Roman Emperor Hadrian built along the basalt crags of the Whin Sill. The distinctive yellow gorse, incidentally, whose bright flowers do particularly well in this part of England, takes its local name from the rock on which it grows, for it is known here as "whin."

The catchment area of the Peak District National Park is by far the biggest. Around ten million people live close to the Park's boundaries, and while it is probably one of the least known among outsiders, local day trippers and picnickers account for large numbers of casual visitors. This Park straddles the northern part of the Midlands but reaches fully into the North Country. Extended, unusually, over several counties, it is something of a misnomer, as it has no outright peak, but rather a high-lying mass of dark gritstone. The name relates most likely to the amount of *pig* farming that once went on here. The gritstone gives a distinctively somber character to many of the villages and country houses within and near the Park's borders.

Two other Parks apart from the North York Moors extend to the coast. On Exmoor the effect is dramatic; in Cumbria it is a more gentle, subtle experience which can make an antidote to the crowded Lake District heartland. Easily the biggest of the National Parks, the Lake District contains within its boundaries England's highest mountains, including Scafell Pike, Helvellyn and Skiddaw, and nearly all of the country's most substantial lakes.

One of the three or four most popular holiday regions in the whole of Britain, the Lake District is notoriously overcrowded, but only at times and in certain places, and anyone prepared to leave their car and walk three or four hundred yards into the hills can be as away-from-it-all as any modern day backwoodsman. It may be the most commercialized of all the National Parks, but even that is only a response to public demand and commercialism tends to be concentrated in two or three large towns. Famous lakes such as Derwentwater and Windermere draw gregarious visitors iike a magnet, and the shores of these two may resemble seaside resorts, but for every honeypot lake there are less significant lakes, not to mention the little tarns that often don't appear on small scale maps.

Exmoor is one of England's best kept secrets, and even vacationers who discover resorts such as Lynton, once popular with the Edwardians and still made attractive by well maintained Edwardian architectural flourishes, may never venture properly into the hinterland. There are several villages worth a stop, among them Dulverton, a toytown place with a large main street that doubles as a market place; Exford, just a couple of inns, a shop or two, a garage and a village green; and Simonsbath, which has the status of a village but little to show for it except a good hotel and a view of meadows, grazing horses and a rippling stream: altogether a tonic for jaded city dwellers. For every traveler acquainted with Exmoor probably ten have experienced Dartmoor to the south. Its southernmost edge goes close to but does not actually reach the coast. Its terrain may be unremarkable in Northumbrian terms but it is nevertheless the biggest expanse of wilderness and untamed moorland in the southern half of England.

A famous feature of Dartmoor is its massive granite "tors," some transformed into bizarre shapes by the weather. Much of Dartmoor is cloaked in heather, but there are many tucked-away boggy places, several of them known for their rare plant life. Dartmoor ponies run wild though they are rounded up every fall. This was once a Royal forest, but before that there were human settlements going back several thousand years: cairns and stone circles are reminders of this period.

Every time a new amusement park is opened in England, or a municipal country park laid down, some voices are raised in opposition. The country, they say, is becoming a glorified museum. Others insist that the National Parks came too late to save "the weeds and the wilderness." But England's seven National Parks are not arid and dead. They have been carefully nurtured so as to be living parts of the whole, just accessible enough to encourage visitors, just wild enough to allow people to get lost if they want to.

Above left Dartmoor, which has been described as "the largest great wilderness in southern Britain". Almost unchanged in its wildest stretches for thousands of years, the moor is notorious for its thick mists and spongy bogs: virtually all of Devon's rivers have their origins on Dartmoor.

Left Clapper Bridge, Postbridge, Devon. Bridges of this type consist of massive granite slabs laid across horizontal piers built up of the same material. Although visitors like to credit these with great antiquity, they are more likely to be medieval than prehistoric.

Borrowdale is some people's favorite Lakeland valley. It is about 15 miles long, from the head of Langstrath to Keswick, and in places more than 4 miles across. The high fells of Borrowdale are as dramatic as any in the Lake District National Park, but the valley is dominant, not the fells, and this increases the appeal for visitors.

The beauty of the Wharfedale landscape, particularly that north of Ilkley, in the Yorkshire Dales National Park, has earned it the accolade of being the finest of the Yorkshire dales. There are many attractive walks and the picturesque ruins of Bolton Abbey, founded on its present site in 1151.

Left Bakewell, Derbyshire, is one of several sizeable but still very appealing towns that lie well within national parks. Roughly equidistant between Buxton, at the Peak District park's north western edge, and Matlock, on the east side, it is bustling but not overrun, pretty but not self-consciously so. It is particularly well known for its "Bakewell puddings", sold locally.

Below The Exmoor National Park is not just the windswept moorland of some holidaymakers' memories, but, in parts, a prosperous farming community. Yet untamed wooded valleys (locally known as "combes") give clues to the location. Even this degree of afforestation can cause concern, for the primeval land is ever under threat from developers and tree-planters, and open, "unproductive" moorland has to be protected.

Right Connoiseurs of dramatic scenery would have to go a long way to beat Malham in the Yorkshire Dales National Park. It has everything a geologist ever dreamed of: superb, raw limestone scenery, the sheer white cliff of Malham Cove — from the bottom of which emerges the River Aire — and, 2 miles away (on foot) the 150 acre lake of Malham Tarn.

Left The Vale of Edale, in the Peak District National Park, lies at the southern end of the Pennine Way — the first continuous long-distance footpath to be opened in Britain. The photograph was taken from Jacob's Ladder, a slightly kinder starting point for the walk than a bleaker alternative when the weather is inclement. The village of Edale is busy and attractive.

Below left Tarn Hows near Coniston in the Lake District National Park is more intimate and accessible than many of the more distinguished lakes. The name "tarn" (several lakes are so called) derives from the old Norse "tjorn", meaning "tear", or "dewdrop" — an evocative description of these generally overlooked large pools.

Below Exmoor in winter. At 265 square miles, Exmoor is the smallest of England's seven national parks, and probably the least known to outsiders.

CHAPTER 5

England-on-Sea

Nowhere in England is more than 70 miles from the sea, and nowhere in Cornwall, for example, which is the proud possessor of two separate and distinctive coastlines, is further than fifteen. But it is not just Sunday excursions to the nearest beach that make for a special relationship between coast and countryside. Inland weather is affected by what happens on the coast, rivers that are a modest trickle in the Cotswolds or the Yorkshire Dales gather momentum as they approach the sea.

It is only (relatively speaking) about 10,000 years since Britain was a promontory of north west Europe. As ice melting at the end of the last great Ice Age raised water levels, Britain became an island. But that was not the end of it, and the coast of England — and Scotland and Wales — is vulnerable and always at the mercy of the pounding sea.

There are a dozen coastal villages in Humberside mentioned in the Domesday Book of 1086 that have now been swallowed by the sea. There are spits of land exposed to everything the weather and the sea can throw at them that may not exist twenty years hence, there are hundreds of square miles of marshland that provide farmers with a living where once there was just water. And it is not just the east coast that is affected in this way: the granite of Cornwall and the limestone of Dorset are vulnerable too. A classic example is Durdle Door, a bizarre and unlikely archway jutting out into the sea, fashioned entirely by the elements.

Brighton's Palace Pier is the only one of that popular and prosperous resort's piers to be intact and open to the public. Erected in Victorian and Edwardian times, piers were seen as a way to experience the ocean at first hand without running the risk of seasickness.

Britain as a whole has over 7000 miles of coastline and no fewer than twenty English counties have their own seaside. As well as Cornwall, both Devon and Norfolk effectively have two, each different in character, each with its prevailing winds and its own loyal following among vacationers.

England's past is closely linked with the sea and seafarers. From King Canute, whose apparent defiance of the waves is said to have been his way of showing his sycophantic courtiers regal fallibility, to Sir Francis Drake, whose game of bowls before setting sail to defeat the Spanish Armada is one of the most enduring symbols of England's one-time naval supremacy, from Lord Nelson to the Normandy landings, English schoolboys have thrilled to stories of the seas that lap England's astonishingly varied coastline.

Regular luxury cruisers circumnavigate the whole of Britain's coastline, negotiating in the process the Pentland Firth between Orkney and the mainland of Scotland, which is said to be among the roughest water in the world. Yachtsmen and cruise passengers enjoy an endlessly changing panorama. From the Elizabethan ramparts of Berwick-upon-Tweed, right on the Scottish border, to the sandy but windswept beaches around Bamburgh, whose great gaunt castle overlooks the North Sea. From the holiday resorts of Scarborough and Whitby, the latter all bright red tiled roofs, screaming gulls and green fishing boats, to the beetling cliffs of Flamborough Head in North Yorkshire, nothing is predictable.

Further down the coast, Skegness, in Lincolnshire, used to be known unofficially as Nottingham-on-Sea, so regularly did

Opposite Towanroath Shaft, Chapel Porth, near St Agnes Head, Cornwall. In the care of the National Trust, this spectacularly positioned tin-mine working is — despite its roofless engine house — still largely intact and sound. Tin was produced here from the underlying stone until the 1920s, when cheap overseas imports made it no longer viable.

Below Though the days of the great transatlantic liners are long past (only the QE2 still plies regularly between Southampton and New York), this city is still a great commercial and passenger port. There are boat tours of the docks and a busy hydrofoil, ferry and hovercraft service bridges the gap between the mainland and the Isle of Wight.

citizens of that once grimy industrial city travel to this part of the east coast for their vacations. Whether at Skegness, Eastbourne or Newquay, nearly every English person lays claim to a piece of the coast, frequently where he or she spent childhood vacations and it is only in recent years that a week at the seaside has ceased to be a part of the social fabric.

Piers are particularly nostalgic: they offer landlubbers a chance of going to sea without all the attendant hassle and, particularly, without being seasick. Not surprisingly, over fifty of them still survive around the coast of Britain, the longest of them at Southend, some of them shabby and down at heel, a slowly increasing number proud and carefully renovated tributes to the Victorians or Edwardians who built them. Among the best is Eastbourne. For most people brought up in England a walk along the pier is a nostalgic trip, past knots of anglers, taffy apple and cotton candy stands, past mahogany colored old women devoted to sea and sun who "wouldn't go abroad if you paid me."

The south coast of England is by far the most populous coast: it has been calculated that about three million people live in under an hour's drive of the resorts between Beachy Head and Selsey Bill: that is Brighton and Hove, Worthing, Littlehampton, Bognor Regis, as well as lesser known places like Rottingdean, Shoreham and Seaford. Fortunately the nature of the coastline means that tens of thousands can be absorbed without detriment, and if the sands do get too crowded or the sun gets too hot (it is not unknown!) the breezy South Downs are never far away. To the west lie Bournemouth, a prosperous and elegant town that absorbs thousands of beach fanciers without any loss of dignity, and the Dorset coast.

Between Dartmouth and Plymouth in Devon, the South Hams jut out into the sea like a cow's udder, an unromantic description for one of coastal Devon's most romantic locations. Plymouth, the county's famous maritime city, is historic but bears the scars of unsympathetic modernization.

Below About twenty-five nineteenth-century Thames sailing barges still survive, and one of the rarest and most enjoyable maritime experiences is to take a day trip or even an all-found holiday in one. In Dickens's time these handsome boats carried hay, bricks, manure and other cargoes down the Thames and round the coast, particularly to the rivers Blackwater (in Essex) and Medway (in Kent). They are a reminder of the days when London's Dockland teemed with maritime activity.

Left The harbor at Scarborough, North Yorkshire, is distinguished by the parrot-green livery of its many fishing boats and no visit to this lively all-purpose seaside resort is complete without a walk around the moorings. Traditionally Scarborough was the smartest family resort: as you moved up the social scale you left more southerly Yorkshire resorts behind.

Below The chalky promontory of Flamborough Head, Humberside, was once a fortress and lookout post, though that proved no serious challenge to Viking invaders around 700 AD. In 1779 local residents watched a battle off the headland between the colonist John Paul Jones and two English warships, but nowadays nothing is as dramatic as life in the teeming colonies of gulls and guillemots.

But all of these traditionally play second fiddle among vacationers to almost anywhere in Cornwall, south or north. Cornwall's south coast is loosely known as the Cornish Riviera. It extends roughly from Polperro and Looe in the east to Land's End in the west, a distance of about 100 miles. There are rocky coves and sandy beaches, green headlands from which to watch the sunset in the cool of the evening, fishing villages and more substantial resorts. The River Tamar all but separates Cornwall from the rest of England, and some Cornish people would be delighted if the severance was complete.

The north of Cornwall is more rugged and generally more windy, but it has its enthusiasts, not least among whom are surfers. Widemouth Bay, whose name is descriptive, is a surfers' resort in its own right. Further east the Cornish coast gives way to Devon's second coast – appropriately known as North Devon. It is tortuous enough, but its contours are softened by rich woodland reaching down to the water's edge. At the approach to Bristol and the River Severn mud and silt take over: apart from Weston-super-Mare, a classic of its kind, there are few resorts.

Torquay, Newquay and Weston-super-Mare have to acknowledge the supremacy of Lancashire's Blackpool, the flamboyant, self-assertive queen of traditional vacation spots. But in contrast, just a few miles to the north, are the dangerous, impressive, shifting sands of Morecambe Bay which have tempted many a walker and drowned him when the tides sweep across the sand and treacherous mud.

Taking a guided tour is the most reliable way to see this remarkable natural feature, from which, when conditions are not misty, the southerly hills of the Lake District are clearly visible.

Left Lulworth Cove, Dorset. Vulnerable to the ravages of the sea and the elements, the limestone cliffs and shingle beaches of the Dorset coast have an irresistible lure for high season vacationers. The best known feature along this part of the coast is Durdle Door, a limestone arch wrought by the constant attention of wind and weather. In time that arch will lose its top, leaving just pillars.

Right St Michael's Mount. Like a smaller version of Mont St Michel, in northern France, this great Cornish landmark is connected to the mainland by a causeway. When that is covered by water, visitors can cross by boat from Penzance or Marazion. There are guided tours of the castle, which has had a chequered and sometimes violent history.

Further north still, the Cumbrian coast is probably best approached via the narrow gauge Eskdale to Ravenglass railway. Ravenglass has a low key, subtle beauty. In contrast the great sandstone cliffs of St. Bees Head, within the same county, and more reminiscent of the dramatic scenery inland, rise sheer out of the water to a height of 300 feet.

Left Fisherman at Dunwich, on the Suffolk coast. An acquired taste for vacationers, this part of East Anglia is windswept and the beaches pebbly, but fresh cod and plaice, frequently available for sale on the beach, and the subtle low-key beauty of estuary and marsh, added to the call of wildfowl, is seductive and beautiful.

Below Shoreham-by-Sea, West Sussex, is something of a seaside resort but also a workaday town. For several hundred years it has been a port, and coasters and colliers still use it. Old Shoreham is especially worth seeing, where the parish church is partly Saxon, partly Norman. The Marlipins Museum, located in a Norman building, is devoted to local history.

Boiling cockles and whelks at a Norfolk fishing port. These traditional low-cost day-tripper's seaside foods, though found in gourmet restaurants, are usually sold cooked and shelled. Piquant and full of protein, these shellfish are usually eaten cold and with vinegar or sometimes in dishes in place of mussels or oysters. They are best when there is the letter "r" in the month.

For every visitor to Ravenglass, perhaps a thousand others go to Blackpool or Scarborough, which suits the seeker after solitude. It means that it is possible to find an almost deserted cove on Labor Day, and it means that England's traditional, boisterous resorts still have a following and will not die. In some places the sea is almost incidental, in others it is a continual presence. It has the novelty of cutting ordinary mortals down to size, and this must have something to do with the very particular outlook on the world that island people have – the English included.

Opposite Clovelly, whose whitewashed houses contrast with the heavily wooded hillside typical of the underoccupied Devon coast, is perhaps the most photographed village in Devon — though rarely from this angle. Donkeys carry weary visitors up the steep climb from the sea to the car park above.

Below Bosham, West Sussex, at the head of a tributary of the Chichester Channel, has played a significant part in English history: there was a Roman settlement; King Canute made his stand here against the waves; and it was from these shores that King Harold set off for a meeting — about two years prior to the 1066 invasion — with William of Normandy.

Things to see in England

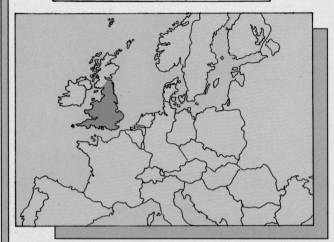

Chawton, Hampshire

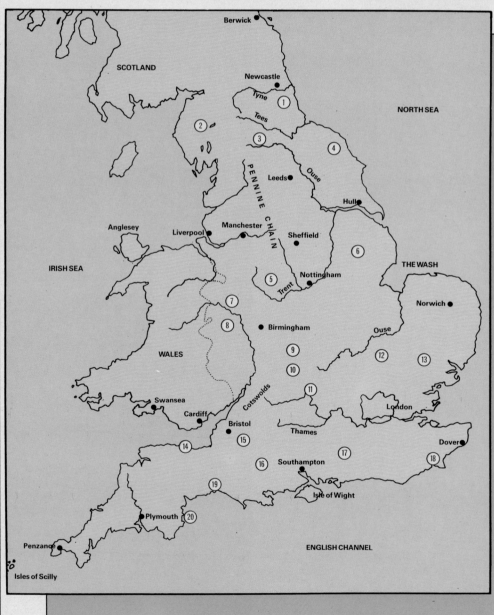

1. Beamish, County Durham
Once the location of a small coalmine and a country house in pleasant surroundings, Beamish is now one of the largest open-air museums in England with entire streets of Victorian shops and miners' cottages, a tram and railroad system, and farm.

2. Grasmere, Cumbria
A village on the green valley floor beside Lake Grasmere, overlooked by Helvellyn and the Langdale Pikes. William Wordsworth lived at Dove Cottage for nine years and was succeeded there by Thomas de Quincy.

3. Hawes, North Yorkshire
This grey little town in Upper Wensleydale, with a stream cascading through its eastern end, is noted for its sheep sales. About a mile and a half to the north is Hardrow Force, a splendid waterfall.

4. Goathland, North Yorkshire
The enchanting villages of the North York Moors are well worth a day or two's acquaintance. Goathland can be reached by the steam-operated North Yorkshire Moors Railway, which connects Pickering with British Rail at Grosmont.

5. Ashbourne, Derbyshire
A delightful market town and a good center from which to explore Dovedale and the surrounding hill country. Stoke-on-Trent, Chatsworth, Sudbury Hall and Hardwicke Hall are also an easy day's excursion.

6. Lincoln, Lincolnshire
Seen from most parts of Lincoln is its superbly located cathedral, with many claims to be the most magnificent in all England. The medieval castle should also be visited, while the town also has a good theater, a folk museum and a well-known racecourse.

7. Ironbridge, Shropshire
Regarded by many historians as the cradle of Britain's Industrial Revolution, the Ironbridge Gorge is now the center of an outstanding working museum. It was here in 1709 that iron was first smelted with coke, and 70 years later the world's first metal bridge was constructed across the River Severn.

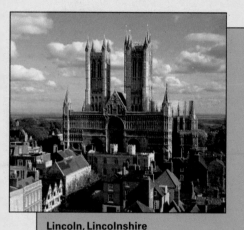

Lincoln, Lincolnshire

Grasmere, Cumbria

8. Ludlow, Hereford and Worcester

Once a major military base for the control of the Welsh borderlands, Ludlow still possesses the ruins of a fine medieval castle. Splendid main-street and plentiful back lanes provide enchanting walks, while superb wooded countryside lies close to the town.

9. Stratford-upon-Avon, Warwickshire

Even if William Shakespeare had not lived in this market town, it would still be a tourist attraction for the River Avon, the historic buildings and the gentle countryside around.

10. Chipping Campden

A perfect center from which to explore the Cotswolds, Chipping Campden is an example of a small town of largely sixteenth- and seventeenth-century buildings which have survived partly because the town's main industry – wool – declined in the late seventeenth century.

11. Oxford, Oxfordshire

Worldwide, for academic tradition and excellence, Oxford has few equals. Besides this, it is a flourishing commercial city – with the atmosphere of a glorified Cotswold market town – and a forest of spires that grace the skyline.

12. Ashwell, Hertfordshire

Amid the rolling parkland and farmland of Hertfordshire this village has a fourteenth-century church with a striking tower; inside, interesting local tapestries are displayed. The "Town House", now a village museum, is one of many good houses in the attractive main street.

13. Long Melford, Suffolk

The village green here is of exceptionally large size and beautifully bordered at its upper end by Elizabethan almshouses and a Perpendicular church. Medieval pageants are held each year at Long Melford Hall.

14. Minehead, Devon

Many visitors to this former fishing settlement miss the upper town, where the nineteenth-century holiday homes give way to winding cobbled streets and color-washed houses.

15. Bath, Avon

Natural hot springs made this a fashionable spa ever since Roman times. Its great period of growth was in the eighteenth century and the steep sides of the town's bowl-shaped valley are lined with tier upon tier of Georgian crescents, terraces and squares.

16. Stonehenge and Avebury, Wiltshire

These collections of huge standing stones confer a peculiar sense of mystery and dignity upon the visitor. The stones yield unmistakeable proof of an intense interest in astronomy and the sun, but one can only guess at the nature of the ceremonies performed in these places.

17. Chawton, Hampshire

Jane Austen moved to the tranquil village of Chawton in 1809. It was during her eight years in Chawton Cottage – now Jane Austen's House – that she completed the final versions of her six novels.

18. Rye, Kent

A port of fluctuating fortunes since the mid-eleventh century, Rye's main industry is now tourism, helped by the many old buildings and the town's association with the American writer Henry James, who lived in Lamb House from 1898 until his death in 1916.

19. Lyme Regis, Dorset

Regularly used as a movie location, this enchanting seaside resort was the setting for John Fowles' novel The French Lieutenant's Woman.

20. Dartmouth, Devon

Overlooked by the world-famous Royal Naval College, Dartmouth is a gem at the head of the Dart Estuary, with steep, largely wooded hills on all sides and two fifteenth-century forts to guard the harbor entrance.

Stonehenge and Avebury, Wiltshire

Ironbridge, Shropshire

The coast of Northumberland is protected from the effects of modern development, and tends to be a secret that northerners keep to themselves. That seductive combination of wide sandy beaches and rocky foreshore that make it hard to get small boys home in time for tea, and the chance of seeing seals and rare seabirds, cast a powerful spell.

PICTURE CREDITS